Content

Lauren Dean & Emily Pollard (9)   34
Luke Windsor (8)   35
Connor Graves (9)   36
Joseph Tait (8)   37
Kian Weatherhogg (8)   38
Luqman Rahman (9)   39
Rahela Sultana (9)   40
Lauren Dean (8)   41
Alex Dean (8)   42
Tia Fudge (8)   43
Rohan Patel (9)   44
Sophie Peters (9)   45
Emily Pollard (9)   46
Jasmine Pontin (8)   47
Akmalur Rahman (8)   48
Kieran Gillott (9)   49
David Fraser (8)   50
Owen Slipp (9)   51
Fahim Chowdhury (9)   52
Liam Brown (9)   53
Mollie Slater (9)   54
Ryehan Amir (9)   55

Limpsfield Junior School, Sheffield

Jake Hutchinson (10)   56
Chad Colton (9)   57
Brandon Chadwick (10)   58
Shumirai Zhuwankinyu (10)   59
Vaughan Peters (10)   60
Abdul Sillah (9)   61
Bailey Briggs (10)   62
Daniel Thorpe (10)   63

Longroyde Junior School, Brighouse

Joe D'Ambrogio (11)   64

St Andrew's CE Primary School, Leasingham

Lauren Berrick (8)   65
Natasha Barton & Kieran Boyle (10)   66
Sydney Mawer (9)   67

St Mary's CE Primary School, Barnsley

Caroline Todd (10)	68
Harry Wilson (10)	69
Liam Travis (10)	70
Eden Lee (9)	71
Sophie White (9)	72
Bethany Green (10)	73
Daniel Jenkinson (10)	74
Martha Isobel Parkinson (9)	75
Harrison Brook (10)	76
Ciaran Reynolds (9)	77
Niall Egan (10)	78
Willem Fisher (10)	79
Isobel Oliver-Haste (10)	80
Oliver Roscoe (10)	81
Katie Phillips (10)	82
Robert Mitchell (10)	83
Jodie Higgins (10)	84
Heather Venson (9)	85
Callum Gillott (10)	86
Jessica Nixon (10)	87

St Joseph's Catholic Primary School, Keighley

Chelsea Bray (8)	88
Libby Todd (7)	89
Oliver Marsh (8)	90
Amy Stoop (8)	91
Amy Thornton (8)	92
Tegan Devlin (8)	93
Saira Ali (7)	94
Anthony Beckwith (7)	95
Hannah Greenwood (8)	96
Samantha Hinchcliffe (7)	97
Kieron Blakeley (8)	98
Niamh McGlynn (7)	99
Ryan Ayers (8)	100
Sean Scully (11)	101
Eve Kendall (11)	102
Sam Vickers (11)	103

Emily McSharry (10)	104
Louise Evans (10)	105
Niamh Hargreaves (11)	106
Libby Cross (11)	107
Emily Harrison (11)	108
Nagina Ditta (11)	109
Terri Moseley (11)	110
Amy De Belder (10)	111
Sophie Dearden (11)	112
Savannah Horsfall (11)	113
Hayley Kit (11)	114
Ihtisham Ahmed (10)	115
Kye Plover (10)	116
Georgia Harrison (11)	117
Lewis Feather (10)	118
Aneesa Parvais (10)	119
Jamie Sharples (11)	120
Kirstie Goodchild (8)	121
Chloe Carr (8)	122
Jennie-Lee Roberts (7)	123
Katie Nash (8)	124
Max Moseley (8)	125
Ryan Henry (8)	126
Taylor Hardaker (8)	127
Bill Narey (8)	128

Towngate Primary School, Ossett

Sophie Kershaw (11)	129
Ben Cornell (11)	130
Daisy Kennedy (11)	131
Jessica Allatt (11)	132
Kate Priestley (10)	133
Joseph Exley (10)	134
Jessica Taylor (11)	135
Nicola Fox (10)	136
Emma Bolton (11)	137
Megan Downes (11)	138
Lauren Ekert (10)	139
Lewys Irvin (11)	140

Alex Coy (11)	141
Phoebe Shore (9), Ella Lamming & Katie Malik (8)	142
Natalia King & Luke England (9)	143
Shannon McGroggan (9) & Bethany Wilbert (8)	144
Sam Hewitt & Ryan Strafford (9)	145
Adam Wheeler & Harry Strafford (8)	146
Molly Maw (8) & Natalie Gregson (9)	147
Arran Senior, Holly Saynor & Jaya Sharma (9)	148
Chloe Stanley, Kelsey Lambourn & Emily Hudson (9)	149
Chloe Smith (7)	150
Samuel Beaumont (8)	151
Sean Owram (8)	152
Harmony Tavakoli (8)	153
Abigail Hemingway (8)	154
Ella Walker (8)	155
Rebecca Hobson & Joshua Callaghan (8)	156
Bethany Cooper (8)	157
Jordan Grace (8)	158
Kelsey Johnson (9)	159
Alana King (10)	160
Darcie Hill (9)	161
Nathan Wilby (9)	162
Kieran Shields (10)	163
Molly Strafford (10)	164
Benjamin Black (10)	165
Alexander Remmer (9)	166
Liam Senior (10)	167
Luke Churchill (10)	168

Weaverthorpe CE Primary School, Malton

Emma Heslington (11)	169
Alex Rough (10) & Louis Hopper (9)	170
James Ireland (9)	171
Mollie Beresford (8)	172
Georgia Tiffany (9)	173
Maisie Thomson (10)	174
Katie Botterill (10)	175
Phoebe Pickering (8)	176
Megan Stubbings (9)	177
Gabriella Fisher (10)	178

Wold Newton School, Driffield

The Poems

Tigers Should Be Safe!

Tiger! Tiger! in your den
Hiding from the hunting men,
How could we be such killing beasts
And eat you for a lovely feast?

How far away we are from you?
Trembling in the mud too.
Everywhere I look I see
Killing for a giant fee.

And what your beauty, what your shape
Running in your golden cape,
And what you fear
We're coming near.

Your tiger's roar,
It shook the floor
And in the air
They just don't care.

Draw your last ever breath
And say hello to your death,
Hunters put down their spears,
As you cry salty tears,
They all have their last sneers.

Tiger! Tiger! in your den
Hiding from the hunting men,
How could we be such killing beasts
And eat you for a lovely feast?

Emily Ayres (11)
Bardney Primary School, Lincoln

Good World Gone Bad

If we don't want war, why fight?
If we don't want climate change, why waste?
We can help, we can shine the light,
If we just weren't in haste.

If we don't like litter why not recycle?
If we don't want pollution, let's energy save.
Don't use the car, we can cycle,
We can do it, just be brave.

Our world is falling apart,
We've got to help eventually,
It's breaking lots of hearts,
But we need to help, essentially.

Alice Mundy (10)
Bardney Primary School, Lincoln

Save The Tigers

Tiger, tiger in his house,
Needs to be quiet as a mouse,
A hunting group is after him,
I'm afraid the hunters may well win.

Why use a knife? Why use a gun?
Why do people find murder fun?
Then I heard the tiger roar,
And I knew the hunters were frauds.

All the tigers must run fast,
As they will soon be in the past,
In the distance I can see,
A frightened tiger staring at me.

Lauren Key (11)
Bardney Primary School, Lincoln

Tiger

Tiger, tiger running wild,
In the night so mild.
With blood streaming from his thigh
Surely he's going to die.

Is there anyone worldwide,
Who can help this tiger's hide?
Or to make him live on and on,
Surely soon he will be gone.

Can this tiger leave his home,
Nowhere left for him to roam.
Will this animal live one day,
Or will the humans get their way?

Here the tiger is lying down,
Resting on his face, a frown.
When will the shooting stop?
There's so much blood, we need a mop.

His life is gone, it won't be long
The tiger's eyes close,
No more air comes through his nose.

Michael O'Sullivan (11)
Bardney Primary School, Lincoln

Peace

Peace is a dolphin
Blue and grey
As beautiful as the sunset
Driven away.

It is the gate of Heaven
Where the dolphins jump over
Silently.

Peace is an angel's heart.

It's a promise I will never break.

Chanel Cox (10)
Castleton Primary School, Leeds

God's Creation

A is for animals,
    creatures big and small.
B is for bubbles,
    rising higher than us all.
C is for clouds,
    soft candy and all white.
D is for desert,
    all beautiful and bright.
E is for elephants,
    all stamping and loud with pride.
F is for flamingoes,
    standing pink side by side.
G is for gardens,
    full of beautiful grass.
H is for happiness,
    that we all hate to pass.
I is for igloo,
    made of solid ice.
J is for jungle,
    as it's hot like nice rice.
K is for kite
    as it soars through the air.
L is for life,
    and it begins right there.
M is for minds,
    what we all have in our heads.
N is for nest,
    that stays there lying dead.
O is for octopus,
    all happy on his own.
P is for Pacific,
    silent waves as its home.
Q is for the Queen,
    a special person she can be.
R is for roads
    so listen, look and see.
S is for summer,
    how hot you can bet.

T is for trees,
how tall can they get?

U is for universe,
where the planets spin away.

V is for valley,
where the quiet people stay.

W is for water
it flows down the river.

X is for xylophone,
if you hit it wrong it makes you shiver.

Y is for youngsters,
beautiful children there are.

Z is for zebra,
they're scared when lions go *raah!*

Simon Blackburn (9)
Castleton Primary School, Leeds

If I Had Wings

(Based on 'If I Had Wings' by Pie Corbett)

If I had wings I would touch the heavens and glide through
                                        the breezy clouds.
If I had wings I would taste the ice-cold stars.
If I had wings I would listen to the space station beeping.
If I had wings I would breathe in the clouds' breath.
If I had wings I would gaze at the clouds moving round the Earth.
If I had wings I would dream of touching the stars.

Matthew Stokes (10)
Castleton Primary School, Leeds

All In The Mind

Peace is a puppy
Black and brown
As beautiful as the moonlight
Drifting through the night.

It is the gate of Heaven
Falling from the sky
So shiny and bright.

It is a promise of God
What he always gives.

It is a kind of angel
Up in the sky
Like a shooting star
On a gentle night.

Jonathan Wright (10)
Castleton Primary School, Leeds

God's Creation

A is for animals
  great creatures one and all,
B is for brightness,
  like the sun that will never fall.
C is for colour
  that the rainbow takes in.
D is for dolphins
  this is where they swim.
E is for Earth
  the planet we live on.
F is for flowers
  in the winter there's none.
G is for God
  the man that got us here.
H is for happiness
  it gets rid of the fear.
I is for igloo
  all shiny but quite cold.
J is for jungle
  it will never get old.
K is for kindness
  the emotion we all share.
L is for love
  the kind that makes us care.
M is for moon
  a circle in the sky.
N is for night
  great place to see a sight
O is for oak
  a tree we all can see,
P is for people
  we all are, even me.
Q is for queen
  a lady who rules you.
R is for recycle
  it's something we should do
S is for summer
  it's the best season ever.

T is for trees
they change during the weather.
U is for universe
where the planets will stay.
V is for violet
a colour not so grey.
W is for wind
it blows along the farm.
X is for xylophone
an instrument played calm.
Y is for youngsters
the future of tomorrow.
Z is for zebras
in a line they all follow.

Roush Abdoubaki (10)
Castleton Primary School, Leeds

Joy/Sadness

Joy
Joy is bright yellow.
It tastes like a beautiful flower.
It smells like fresh cut grass
Joy looks like a newborn puppy.
It sounds like people laughing.
It feels as soft as cotton wool.
Joy is exciting.

Sadness
Sadness is the dullest black.
It tastes like mushy peas.
It smells like a swamp.
Sadness looks like a big empty house.
It sounds like a funeral.
It feels like sloppy mud.
Sadness is scary.

Matthew Hirst (10)
Castleton Primary School, Leeds

Litter

A pple cores all over the floor.
B anana skins rotting away, leaving a horrid smell.
C hewing gum is so, so sticky it goes everywhere.
D on't be so dirty, put litter in the bin.
E mpty cans, broken bottles, so dangerous you can hurt yourself.
F ight for your streets.
G o and keep your streets clean.
H elp to clean the streets.
I will do it for my streets so you do it for yours.
J ust help by putting your rubbish in the bin.
K eep on helping.
L ooks dirty, people shouldn't be so lazy.
M essy, dirty, smelly.
N asty and disgusting.
O range peel rotting away.
P lease be clean.
Q uiet, clean streets we like.
R emember to be not so lazy.
S weet wrappers smell yucky.
T ry, try, all you need to do is try.
U nderstand, do you understand?
V ery clean we should be.
W hat are you going to do about it?
X - I would be very cross with you if you said no to tidying the streets.
Y ou should never say no as we need to keep Britain clean.
Z oos are clean so you should keep your streets clean.
   Remember do not litter.

Caitlin Kitchen (9)
Castleton Primary School, Leeds

Oceans

Oceans are shiny
Silky and clean
Under the ocean
Find what you see
Tell me everything
What did you see?
I saw fish, crabs, eels, everything,
It was fantastic
Let's go again.

Hannah Ryder (10)
Castleton Primary School, Leeds

Wings

(Based on 'If I Had Wings' by Pie Corbett)

If I had wings,
I would touch,
The scorching sun,
And glide down on the greyest cloud.

If I had wings,
I would taste,
The fiery curry and rice.

If I had wings,
I could hear,
The flames rising higher.

If I had wings,
I could smell the burning flames.

If I had wings,
I would,
Gaze at people.

If I had wings,
I would dream of
Staying in the flames,
And seeing the
Rest of the fantastic birds.

Josh Pritchard (9)
Castleton Primary School, Leeds

Peace

Peace is a rabbit.
White and brown.
As fluffy as clouds.

It is angels' wings,
Gliding down from the sky.

Peace is a chocolate bar.
Melting in the summer sun.
As watery as the juice from an apple.

It is a fingertip of Heaven.
In the beautiful fresh sky
Like a shooting star.

Billy Smith (10)
Castleton Primary School, Leeds

Love And Sadness

Love
Love is the red cherry pie.
It tastes like a sweet, soft as ever.
It smells like coconut sponge with custard.
Love looks like a red tulip.
It sounds like a song thrush singing early in the morning.
It feels like a tropical world full of butterflies.
Love is powerful!

Sadness
Sadness is grey like clouds,
Sadness tastes like saltwater,
It smells like dust and cobwebs.
Sadness looks like a puppy locked up in a chain.
It sounds like a newborn baby crying,
It feels like a hard smack.
Sadness is people!

Summer Thomson (10)
Castleton Primary School, Leeds

Happiness

Happiness is a glorious prize given from the heavens.
It looks like two pearly white parts connecting together.
It smells like fresh roses drifting you off in a daydream of happiness.
It tastes like chocolate hearts with the caramel dripping in your mouth,
with a touch of strawberries lifting your heart
to the occasion of joy,
with a scent of aromas from beyond the chocolate.
It feels smooth with a bit of a solid touch like trophies
feeling valuable and rewarding.
Happiness lives in all of us!

Bradley Lawson (10)
Castleton Primary School, Leeds

Saving Our Great Planet!

If you really care about the world
You might want to stop littering
For all the gas that pollutes the sky
In a couple of years the birds might not fly.
If you ever drop a can, all this is because of your hands.
What I mean by littering is pollution, poverty
and the world going brown.
As the tiger is nearly extinct,
I am sat in my chair having a think.
The tiger is on its last legs due to poaching, hunting
and their habitats being destroyed.
So if you want the world to live some more
I suggest that you ditch the car and walk!

Molly Morrell (8)
Fountains CE Primary School, Ripon

Save The Planet

Think about the world and recycle.
Then make the world have a smile.
Have a go to save our planet.
Think all your litter goes straight to your bins.
Straight away like a big heap of hay.
Just say to people, 'No! No! No!'
Save our planet, recycle . . .
Have a go!

Roscoe Savage (9)
Fountains CE Primary School, Ripon

Litter

Litter, litter, litter
Is bad for the environment
Gets thrown away after a few minutes
Spoiling nature.

Litter, litter, litter
Killing lots of animals
People pick it up
Gets thrown away again
Litter, litter, litter.

Sophie Spick (9)
Fountains CE Primary School, Ripon

Recycle Now!

R ecycle now!
E nd throwing away,
C ans and tins,
Y ou don't need plastic bags,
C an't you use a bag for life?
L ive in a world that's safe,
I f you help the world,
N o harm will happen
G et together and help the world!

Alicia Micklefield (9)
Fountains CE Primary School, Ripon

This Beautiful Planet

The world, the world, what a beautiful place.
The world, the world, it's a danger that we face.
The world, the world, it's dying as we speak,
The world, the world, it's starting to leak.
If we all did our bit to save this planet,
It would live forever,
And we wouldn't have to panic.

Sophie Ryan (9)
Fountains CE Primary School, Ripon

Save The World

S ave your energy.
A lways save water.
V acuum less, dust more, or don't make any mess at all.
E nergy, save energy.

T urn off your television.
H elp save energy.
E nergy, save energy.

W alk to school.
O rganic is good.
R ecycle when you can.
L eave your car at home.
D o your best.

Charlotte Evans (8)
Fountains CE Primary School, Ripon

Animals

Animals, animals, beautiful animals, we should save them.
Hedgehogs, birds, dogs and cats, do you really want to kill them?
Think of the penguin, its habitat melting, you could save them!
It's not hard to be friendly to the Earth.

Imogen Hey (8)
Fountains CE Primary School, Ripon

Animals

A whale is a big animal.
We are killing the poor animals.
With plastic bags.

A jellyfish is a wobbly animal.
Jellyfish are mistaking the plastic bags for food!

A turtle has a hard back.
Turtles are putting their heads in the bags.
They get stuck and die.

Emma Sorby (8)
Fountains CE Primary School, Ripon

Animals And Extinction

Who wants to save the animals?
Who likes bats?
Because I like cats.
Some are dying.
Some are mice.
I have a dog.
I have not seen a hedgehog.
I like hares and polar bears.
Why are they becoming extinct?
Where are the animals now?

Rebecca Firenyi (7)
Fountains CE Primary School, Ripon

Litter

L ots of litter ruins the world.

I t's important to not litter.

T he world does not need litter.

T ins are a type of litter.

E arth is falling apart because of litter.

R ings from cans are a type of litter.

Lauren Baird (8)
Fountains CE Primary School, Ripon

Recycling

R ainforests get chopped down for paper.
E xtinction of animals and
C limate change.
Y ou could help too.
C reatures from
L and and sea get
I njured.
N asty gases pollute the air
G et recycling now!

Fraser Abbott (8)
Fountains CE Primary School, Ripon

Our World

The world, the world
The fantastic, beautiful, amazing world
And we are destroyed without it
The sun, the sun
The wonderful sun
The heat, the colour, the amazing sun
We would die without it.
We are destroying the world
We will die soon if you do not act.
Act now!

James Thomas (9)
Fountains CE Primary School, Ripon

Litter

Litter looks like the dark sewers down below us.
Litter sounds like garbage getting scattered on the ground.
Litter feels like bin bags being thrown down on me.
Litter tastes like old, mouldy, gone-off milk.
Litter smells like a dirty hamster's cage.

If only people were more careful our planet would:

Look like a garden full of roses.
Sound like beautiful music.
Feel like the sun's warmth.
Taste like a beefburger.
Smell like doughnuts at a circus.

Kyle Leaning (9)
Henderson Avenue Primary School, Scunthorpe

Conversation With A Tree

Child: 'What can you see, old tree?'
Tree: 'Birds nesting high on me,
At night I see the owl fly above me,
But . . . all the smoke is suffocating.'

Child: 'What can you hear, my friend?'
Tree: 'I hear the laughter in the wind of the children,
Baby animals climbing in my long wide branches,
But . . . I can hear the chainsaw getting closer.'

Child: 'What do you feel, tall tree?'
Tree: 'I feel happy as children are having picnics under me,
I feel the wrinkles of my old age
But . . . anger as the chainsaw puts me to death.'

Lauren Kirk Chapman (9)
Henderson Avenue Primary School, Scunthorpe

Conversation With A Tree

Child: 'What can you see?'
Tree: 'A bird's giant nest just above me,
Children playing happily all around me,
Bulldozers raging all around me.'
Child: 'What can you hear?'
Tree: 'Cars revving on the road,
Children's laughter all around me,
Chainsaws raging all around me.'
Child: 'What can you hear?'
'Breeze hitting me,
The wind whistling all around me,
The chainsaws cutting me down.'

Jordan Embling (8)
Henderson Avenue Primary School, Scunthorpe

Litter

Litter looks like a smelly, overflowing bin.
Litter sounds like a tin rolling around in the wind.
Litter feels like dirty gum stuck on my shoe.
Litter tastes like unwashed socks.
Litter smells like a horrible sewer.

If only we would think about our planet a bit more.

Looks like trees being reborn,
Sounds like birds singing in the sky.
Feels like my soul being released into the fresh air.
Tastes like melting chocolate eggs.
Smells like a lovely rose.

Lauren Dean & Emily Pollard (9)
Henderson Avenue Primary School, Scunthorpe

Litter

Litter looks like hailstones.
Litter sounds like crackling tins.
Litter feels like blood.
Litter tastes like some grubs.
If only people were more careful our planet would:
Look like air fresheners.
Sound like crowds cheering.
Taste like melted chocolate.
Feel like peace and quiet.
Smell like cut grass.

Luke Windsor (8)
Henderson Avenue Primary School, Scunthorpe

Litter

Litter looks like dirty raw sewage in the sea.
Litter sounds like an explosion.
Litter feels like slimed glue.
Litter tastes like baked beans.
Litter smells like a whiffy pint of milk.

If only people were more careful our planet would:
Look like a garden full of flowers
Sound like a robin chirping.
Feel like my dad's beard
Taste like creamy cheese
Smell like my mum's cooking.

Connor Graves (9)
Henderson Avenue Primary School, Scunthorpe

Litter!

Litter looks like suffocating smoke
Litter sounds like a rusty car engine
Litter feels like hard stones in my shoe
Litter tastes like a rotten apple
Litter smells like a fuming bonfire

If only people were more careful our planet would:

Look like a beautiful sunny day
Sound like birds singing sweetly
Feel like the sun shining down on me
Taste like Dairy Milk chocolate
Smell like roses and daffodils.

Joseph Tait (8)
Henderson Avenue Primary School, Scunthorpe

Rubbish

R usty old bike
U gly pile of bin bags
B ottles smashed
B ad smell
I t could make you ill
S ad sight to see
H ope we can clean it up.

Kian Weatherhogg (8)
Henderson Avenue Primary School, Scunthorpe

Conversation With A Tree

Child: 'Wise old tree, what do you see?'

Tree: 'I see a man under my shade,
I see a girl in the sandpit playing with a spade,
I see happy birds, but their smiles are starting to fade.'

Child: 'Enormous tree, what can you hear?'

Tree: 'I hear squirrels laughing together,
I hear a hedgehog shuffling a feather,
I hear a chainsaw like stormy weather.'

Child: 'Most clever tree, what do you feel?'

Tree: 'I feel the rays of the sun against me,
I feel animals sheltering on my knee,
I feel thick yellow smoke suffocating me.'

Luqman Rahman (9)
Henderson Avenue Primary School, Scunthorpe

Litter

Litter looks like millions of specks of dust,
Litter sounds like the garbage man taking the litter away in his truck,
Litter feels like gooey liquid sliding into the pond,
Litter tastes like rotten milk.
Litter smells like mouldy fish.

If people looked after the world, it would:

Look like beautiful gardens,
Sound like birds whistling,
Feel like a mermaid's tail.
Taste like the world's best ice cream,
Smell like a beautiful flower.

Rahela Sultana (9)
Henderson Avenue Primary School, Scunthorpe

Beautiful Tree

'Beautiful tree, what can you see?'

'Animals dancing and running around,
Children having fun in great big fields,
Yellow smoke smoothing and suffocating.'

'Beautiful tree, what can you hear?'

'Birds singing right up high in the sky,
The rustling of leaves,
Chainsaws coming nearer to me.'

'Beautiful tree, what can you feel?'

'Woodpeckers pecking at me,
Squirrels going up and down me,
Chainsaws going through me . . . *Help!*'

Lauren Dean (8)
Henderson Avenue Primary School, Scunthorpe

Enormous Tree

'Enormous tree what can you see?'
'Hunters killing wildlife and dirty cans thrown about.'

'Enormous tree how do you feel?'
'I feel sad to see all my friends being chopped down.'

'Beautiful sky what can you see?'
'Choking chimney smoke coming towards me.'

'Beautiful sky how do you feel?'
'I feel devastated to see the world being destroyed.'

Alex Dean (8)
Henderson Avenue Primary School, Scunthorpe

Litter

Litter looks like an overflowing filth bag made from dirty nappies,
Litter sounds like a garbage truck beeping away.
Litter feels like you're bathing in a swamp full of worms and slugs.
Litter smells so bad there are no words to describe it.
Litter tastes like soggy sprouts.

If people looked after our world it would
Look like a fresh daisy,
Sound like tweeting birds,
Feel like an early morning breeze,
Smell like my mum's perfume,
Taste like delicious chocolate.

Tia Fudge (8)
Henderson Avenue Primary School, Scunthorpe

Litter

Litter looks like an old black cat eating scraps
Litter sounds like two rusty cans banging together
Litter feels like a skip of junk
Litter tastes like a manky slug
Litter smells like out-of-date milk

If only people were more careful our planet would:

Look like a good garden
Sound like birds singing
Feel like a happy wood
Taste like happiness
Smell like sweet fresh air.

Rohan Patel (9)
Henderson Avenue Primary School, Scunthorpe

Litter

Litter looks like spotty chickenpox on your face
Litter sounds like a roaring chainsaw
Litter feels like you are furious inside
Litter tastes like a horrible, mouldy sandwich
Litter smells like your bin after a hot day.

If people were more careful our planet would:

Look like a rosy apple
Sound like birds singing
Feel like you have a friend
Taste like a juicy sweet
Smell like a red rose in a vase.

Sophie Peters (9)
Henderson Avenue Primary School, Scunthorpe

The Tree

'Enchanted tree - what can you see?'

'Colourful birds flying around me,
Some people are having a picnic under my branches,
But I can see the chainsaw getting near to me.'

'Beautiful tree - what can you hear?'

'I can hear squirrels climbing up me,
I can hear caterpillars eating me,
And I can hear the chainsaw two doors away from me.'

'Scorching tree - what can you feel?'

'The sunshine blazing,
Laughter filling the air.

While I am slowly dying.'

Emily Pollard (9)
Henderson Avenue Primary School, Scunthorpe

Litter

Litter looks like a dirty bin,
Litter sounds like somebody scrunching a wrapper,
Litter feels like you have just been thrown into toxic waste,
Litter tastes like ice cream that's been in sand,
Litter smells like foul ear wax.

If only people were more careful our planet would:

Look like a beautiful rose,
Sound like children's laugher
Feel like a soft teddy bear,
Taste like sweets and chocolate,
Smell like a clean house.

Jasmine Pontin (8)
Henderson Avenue Primary School, Scunthorpe

Litter

'Humungous trees, what can you see?'
'Dirty litter at my feet.'

'Enormous tree, how do you feel?'
'Suffocated and unhappy.'

'Salty sea, what can you see?'
'Poisonous rubbish being dumped in me.'

'Wavy sea, how do you feel?'
'Sad to see my sparkly friends destroyed.'

'Helpful child, what do you see?'
'Rubbish being dumped on the planet.'

'Special child, how do you feel?'
'Unhappy to see our planet not being looked after properly.'

Akmalur Rahman (8)
Henderson Avenue Primary School, Scunthorpe

Litter

Litter looks like smelly, scruffy cars crashed together.
Litter sounds like a hard drum banging on the ground.
Litter feels like a sharp pointy tin lid cutting me apart.
Litter tastes like a red and yellow hot, spicy American chilli pepper.
Litter smells like an old dusty dustbin next to you.

If only people were more careful our planet would:

Look like the green and red apples falling off the tree.
Sound like a tune going through my ear.
Feel like wind on a soft green hill.
Taste like pure green apple juice.
Smell like red and pink roses.

Kieran Gillott (9)
Henderson Avenue Primary School, Scunthorpe

Save The Planet

Litter looks like a dusty, horrible street.
Litter sounds like a burning fire crackling in the distance.
Litter feels like icebergs hitting my hands.
Litter tastes like black horrible plastic.
Litter smells like a green, rotten French cheese.

David Fraser (8)
Henderson Avenue Primary School, Scunthorpe

Litter

Litter looks like a dirty, squished landfill.
Litter sounds like a monster truck crushing some cars.
Litter feels like lots of knives all cutting me.
Litter tastes like horrible poison.
Litter smells like revolting, poisonous gas.

If only people were more careful our planet would:

Look like a magical paradise.
Sound like a violin playing a sweet tune.
Feel like a warm swimming pool.
Taste like a cold ice cream on a warm day.
Smell like some sweet raspberries.

Owen Slipp (9)
Henderson Avenue Primary School, Scunthorpe

Litter

Litter looks like horrible, disgusting garbage.
Litter sounds like rumbling thunder.
Litter feels like sharp pointy glass.
Litter tastes like mouldy banana skin.
Litter smells like stinky socks.

If only people cared for our planet it would:

Look like the green countryside.
Sound like the beautiful paradise.
Feel like smooth waters.
Taste like sweet tasty ice cream.
Smell like tasty raspberries.

Fahim Chowdhury (9)
Henderson Avenue Primary School, Scunthorpe

Litter

Litter looks like a horrible dark day.
Litter sounds like horrid music.
Litter feels like sharp, spiky glass.
Litter smells like evil gas.

If only people were more careful our planet would:

Look like a nice place
Sound like a lot of good music.
Feel like the green grass.
Taste like a good banana.
Smell like the fresh air.

Liam Brown (9)
Henderson Avenue Primary School, Scunthorpe

Litter

Litter looks like a dirty, scruffy garden.
Litter sounds like a big storm electrocuting the floor as it falls.
Litter feels like a dirty disgusting drain.
Litter tastes like a mouldy piece of cabbage.
Litter smells like a toxic waste gassing me.

If only people were more careful our planet would:

Look like a beautiful colourful bunch of flowers.
Sound like baby birds singing to their mother.
Feel like a bunch of happy people having fun.
Taste like a nice piece of colourful rock.
Smell like fresh baked sweet bread.

Save our planet!

Mollie Slater (9)
Henderson Avenue Primary School, Scunthorpe

Litter

Litter looks like dirty, scruffy, muddy paper.
Litter sounds like an explosion in the city of Leeds.
Litter feels like disgusting smashed glass.
Litter tastes like old smelly bananas.
Litter smells like intoxicating gas.

If only people were more careful our planet would:

Look like the most beautiful paradise.
Sound like the sky singing sweetly.
Feel like light blue waves.
Taste like cold creamy ice cream on a sunny day.
Smell like delicious hotdogs.

Ryehan Amir (9)
Henderson Avenue Primary School, Scunthorpe

Soldiers At War

Think about the ravenous children crying
While the enemy jets are flying.

Think about the sad soldiers dying
While the bombs are blasting.

Think about the rats biting
While the soldiers are fighting.

Think about the silent suffering
While the citizens are dying.

Jake Hutchinson (10)
Limpsfield Junior School, Sheffield

Death!

Think about . . .
Flying bullets
Blasting bombs killing people
Threatening
People suffering
Pain
Pain
Pain
Shocked people
Suffering soldiers

Think about . . .
Villains' tanks storming through
Lucky armour protecting me
Guns going *bang, bang, bang*.

Chad Colton (9)
Limpsfield Junior School, Sheffield

Catastrophic War

Why do we have war?
Why do we kill people?
Why do we take hostages?
Why do we blow stuff to smithereens?

Why are the fighter jets bombing?
Why are our civilians suffering?
Why are we laying gas down?
Why are we making children cry?

Brandon Chadwick (10)
Limpsfield Junior School, Sheffield

Early Extinction!

Think about . . .
The innocent snow tigers petrified of the poachers.
The desperate whales in the polluted sea.
The furry pandas too tired to walk.

Think about . . .
The magnificent seals being abused for their leather.
The dodos - which are already dead.
The suffering stripy tigers.

Think about . . .
The needless waste of beautiful creatures.
The homeless animals' habitats that are down.
The endless extinction - gone for eternity.

Think about . . .
The oily oceans choking the frightened fish.
The food vanishing instantly.
The catastrophic consequences . . .

Shumirai Zhuwankinyu (10)
Limpsfield Junior School, Sheffield

Think About War!

Think about . . .
The torturing tanks,
The violence to villages,
The suffering to soldiers,

Think about . . .
The flying fighter jets,
The supersonic rockets,
The devastated dying civilians,

Think about . . .
The intolerable intimidations,
The potent poisons,
The helpless hostages.

Think about . . .
Frightful firing guns
The brutal bombs blasting
The crying children.

Vaughan Peters (10)
Limpsfield Junior School, Sheffield

Stop The Chaos Of War

Think about . . .
The innocent poor people dying.
Waking up and crying
Rampaging tanks crashing
Through the quiet neighbourhood
Purposefully causing a furious fire
However some people survive this chaos
And try to have a happy life.

Think about . . .
The poor little babies with no mums and dads because they got shot
Don't let me talk about houses getting burned down.

Think about . . .
A war-torn village, do you think anyone will eat there?
Or live there?
Or swim there?
Please do something about it.

Abdul Sillah (9)
Limpsfield Junior School, Sheffield

War

Think about . . .
The fast jets flying
The children crying
The blasting bombs dropping.

Think about . . .
The suffering soldiers dying
The devastating bombs banging
The mums and dads dying

Think about . . .
The rats spying
The bullets firing
The tanks travelling.

Bailey Briggs (10)
Limpsfield Junior School, Sheffield

Think

Think about . . .
The frightened children crying.
The enemy soldiers spying,
The sad civilians dying,
The fighter planes a-flying.

Think about . . .
The gatling guns,
The squashed sad cherry buns,
The suffering of the wounded nuns,
The total lack of good fun.

Think about . . .
The unfriendly fire,
The horrible, evil tripwire,
The disagreements which are dire,
The disappearance of the messiah.

Think about . . .
The children laughing,
The soldiers gone,
The civilians smiling,
The fighting planes landing to rest.

Think about . . .
The water guns,
The nuns handing out the Bible,
The baker's orders are filled up,
The funny husband back from the war.

Think about . . .
The friendly felines,
The camping trip,
The shaking of hands to change the world,
The reappearance of God.

Daniel Thorpe (10)
Limpsfield Junior School, Sheffield

Litter Is A Disgrace

Litter roams the streets,
Animals are its prey,
It traps them in a deadly way,

Litter comes in disguises,
Hangs about in doorways,
It is seen a lot in the sun's rays.

Litter is as dirty as a cockroach,
Mucks up the town,
Without litter the world would be as clean as the Queen's crown.

Litter deceives the police,
It sneaks away in the gloom,
Climbing up the window into your room.

Joe D'Ambrogio (11)
Longroyde Junior School, Brighouse

Keep The Sky Blue

If you love the world around you
And want to keep the sky blue,
Then start recycling, it's as easy as this.
Pick up all your rubbish and just
Don't throw it away, sort it into bits that can be used another way.
Tomorrow's newspaper is probably what I read today.
Because I put it in my green bin
And these men took it away,
Then probably by Friday it will be back in the shop.
You see this way it means less trees will get the chop
And that's just a small part of what we can do.
So keep recycling and see the difference it makes to you.

Lauren Berrick (8)
St Andrew's CE Primary School, Leasingham

Noises Of The Rainforests

Noises of the rainforests
Hear them out loud,
Noises of the rainforests
Please don't cut them down.

Noises of the rainforests
Hear them talk and sing,
Noises of the rainforests
See the flapping wings.

Noises of the rainforests
Hear the rain drip down,
Noises of the rainforests
Hear the beautiful sounds.

Noises of the rainforests
Hear them out loud,
Noises of the rainforests
Please don't cut them down.

Natasha Barton & Kieran Boyle (10)
St Andrew's CE Primary School, Leasingham

Summer Breeze

Water ripples
And rocks clang.
Grass sways
And leaves hang.
Rivers flow
And sand sprays
In the breeze
Of summer days.

Sydney Mawer (9)
St Andrew's CE Primary School, Leasingham

The World's End

The world around me is full of worry and panic,
Prices of fossil fuels are rising, for we are running out,
Pollution is causing panic, by melting the ice caps above,
The world is in worry but are we doing the right or wrong thing?
By using fossil fuels, even though it will not bother us,
But I feel that we must stop for our children's children will suffer,
We do have renewable energy but we do not use it enough,
I am writing this poem to make a stand
Because we are killing this world.
If you want this world to live for another 2008 years
Then use renewable energy,
But if you don't care about your grandchildren
And carry on using fossil fuels,
Then you could say you are a
Murderer!

Caroline Todd (10)
St Mary's CE Primary School, Barnsley

The Sun

The sun it lights the morning
It lets the flowers grow
It's nature's way of feeding Earth
You'd think that we would know.

To use all nature's ideas
To make us all feel better
No fumes, no fuels, no greenhouse effects
We should just write a letter.

Tell the world to save the Earth
And give us each an hour
Starting with a simple thing
Fitting solar power.

Harry Wilson (10)
St Mary's CE Primary School, Barnsley

The Environment Poem

My environment has lots of trees,
This makes me so happy and very pleased.

My environment has lots of flowers,
I could look at these for hours and hours.

My environment has lots of creatures,
More than my school teachers.

My environment would not exist if
We did not have any of this.

Liam Travis (10)
St Mary's CE Primary School, Barnsley

Weather

Rain, rain
Splashing down
Drip, drip
On the fields and on the town.

Sun, sun
Scorching hot
Shine, shine
Flowers grow in their pots.

Thunder, thunder
Very loud
Bang, clash
Comes from a cloud.

Clouds, clouds
Black and grey
Fluffy, fluffy
Saving water for the next day.

Wind, wind
Sometimes cold, sometimes hot
Whistle, whistle
Blowing through your hair sometimes
When it's hot.

Eden Lee (9)
St Mary's CE Primary School, Barnsley

Animals

A sweet animal will one day be extinct.
N o one should be killing them
I t is important that we help them
M ost of the animals we love will die.
A penguin won't be here
L ove animals
S top killing them.

Sophie White (9)
St Mary's CE Primary School, Barnsley

Say No To Litter!

The world would be a cleaner place,
If litter wasn't dropped,
Should more bins be provided
The problem could be stopped.

The world would be a safer place,
With less rubbish lying around,
People should put it in a bin
Not leave it on the ground.

The world would be a happier place,
If we recycled more,
Rubbish can be used again,
So let's make it the law!

Bethany Green (10)
St Mary's CE Primary School, Barnsley

Endangered Animals

Orange, black and white,
Creeps in the grass,
This we will not see,
Because it's in the past.

It makes me angry,
It makes me sad,
The tiger is being perished
When it should be cherished.

How cruel is mankind,
To kill such a wonderful creature,
For financial gain,
And silly good luck charms.

Daniel Jenkinson (10)
St Mary's CE Primary School, Barnsley

Better Place A Better World

Life on Earth is good,
But in the future it might not be so,
Animals and extinction,
Poverty and climate change
A few of the things
Causing so much concern.

Climate change is our worst concern of all
It spoils animals' habitats,
Melts the ice caps in the Poles,
And it will bring spring early.

Poverty is one of the worst concerns too,
People in parts of Africa need water
But climate change is drying it all up,
So we could act now and help them.

Martha Isobel Parkinson (9)
St Mary's CE Primary School, Barnsley

Pollution

P ollution is bad.
O zone will disappear.
L itter everywhere.
L et people be aware.
U nderstand the world.
T ogether we can work it out.
I , myself and friends.
O pen your eyes and see.
N ow let's hope for the next century.

Harrison Brook (10)
St Mary's CE Primary School, Barnsley

The War

When the war comes,
A storm comes.
Filling the sky with dark clouds.
The soldiers are tired and afraid,
They must carry on the fight,
That stormy sky will turn bright.

When the war is over,
The sky is bright,
The whole of the world
Will be a beautiful sight,
There will be peace, love and harmony,
Those soldiers come home to their family.

Ciaran Reynolds (9)
St Mary's CE Primary School, Barnsley

Weird Weather

It rains so much we have big floods
Nowhere to escape, not even the woods
Rivers burst with unbeatable forces
Some can even run as fast as horses.

When it's sunny it's really nice
Not like in winter with all that ice
We all have fun playing games
But not aware of climate change.

Niall Egan (10)
St Mary's CE Primary School, Barnsley

Pollution! Pollution! What's The Solution?

Pollution is bad,
It makes people ill,
I feel so sad,
Pollution can kill.

It goes in the soil,
It goes in the air,
It makes my blood boil,
Some people really don't care.

Pollution is litter,
It makes such a mess,
Recycling is better,
That makes it much less.

We need to reuse,
What resources we can,
To make it good news,
For the future of man.

Willem Fisher (10)
St Mary's CE Primary School, Barnsley

Recycling For Me And You!

Recycling is the thing to do
It makes the planet better for me and you
Putting your rubbish in different bins
This means the environment really wins
When the rubbish is taken away
It's recycled to make something for another day.

Isobel Oliver-Haste (10)
St Mary's CE Primary School, Barnsley

Litter Lout

Litter, litter everywhere
Litter, litter anywhere
Throw it down, spit it out
There are lots and lots of litter louts.

People should recycle,
Their very, very best.
Or they should get fined
Or punished for their mess.

So let's learn our lesson in the UK
Put it in the bin first
Then walk away.

Oliver Roscoe (10)
St Mary's CE Primary School, Barnsley

Recycle, Recycle

Recycle your papers,
Recycle your tins,
Please place them in appropriate bins,
We must do our share,
To provide cleaner air,
To make planet Earth a wonderful
Environment to share.

Recycle your glass, bottles and jars,
Recycle all rubbish you leave in your car,
Take them to Asda, Morrisons or Tesco,
Or leave them for the Mr Recycle Man
Alfresco!

Katie Phillips (10)
St Mary's CE Primary School, Barnsley

Recycling The Earth

To recycle the Earth,
We have to act now,
We need to stop littering,
We have to do it now.

We will save animals from extinction,
The rainforest needs saving,
Our planet has to be saved,
War needs to be stopped.

You can help us,
All you have to do is,
To recycle forever
And to make less pollution.

Robert Mitchell (10)
St Mary's CE Primary School, Barnsley

Our World

This is a warning!
Fossil fuels are causing global warming,
Fossil fuels and other things cause pollution,
So we need to find a solution!

Recycling our rubbish will help a bit,
That will help animals not to be extinct!
This will help our world to be a nicer place to be,
So make a change for everyone, for all of us to see!

Jodie Higgins (10)
St Mary's CE Primary School, Barnsley

Electricity

Electricity, electricity,
It powers our homes.
Electricity, electricity,
What would we do without it?
Unfortunately, unfortunately,
It is causing pollution
Unfortunately, unfortunately,
It is killing the planet.

Heather Venson (9)
St Mary's CE Primary School, Barnsley

The Rainforest

The rainforest will stun the nation
It's swarming with hunters' infestation
What's worse, it's only for a dime,
Hunting for money, what a selfish crime!

Callum Gillott (10)
St Mary's CE Primary School, Barnsley

Our World

I want you to be environmentally clean.
So the world's the best you've ever seen.
And to help keep the world sweet,
And not smell like sweaty feet.

We need to find a good solution,
To all the world's horrible pollution,
And when I see the world at war,
I think it should be against the law.

You've got bags and boxes,
To put in your smelly socks,
So put your litter in the provided bins.
And remember to recycle your stuff, like tins.

Jessica Nixon (10)
St Mary's CE Primary School, Barnsley

War, War Stop It

War, war, stop it now
War, war what is it for?
For people are dying
It is not fair on their family, they are really upset
We don't like the war.
War is poor, war is sore.
What is it used for?

Chelsea Bray (8)
St Joseph's Catholic Primary School, Keighley

Smoking

Please, please do not smoke
If you do then people will choke
They get poorly and they could die
From all the smoke that they designed
We don't like all the smoke.

Libby Todd (7)
St Joseph's Catholic Primary School, Keighley

This Is The Time

This is the time the war should end
This is the time littering stops.
This is the time stuff should be recycled.
Imagine a poor person with nowt to eat.
Give him the food you don't need.
This is the time animals should be safe.
This is the time all people should not be homeless.
This is the time the climate should change
This is the time pollution stops
I wish all this would stop so the world would be a nice and clean
And better place.

Oliver Marsh (8)
St Joseph's Catholic Primary School, Keighley

Keeping Our World Safe

War, what is it for?
Smoke might make you choke.
Recycling makes you cycle.
Litter makes glitter.
Phoneless makes you homeless.
Pollution makes its own solution.
When animals die it makes me cry!

Amy Stoop (8)
St Joseph's Catholic Primary School, Keighley

Keep Our World Clean

What is it like to be homeless?
Well it's just hopeless.

Never smoke, it makes you choke.
War, what is it for?

Ban your motorbike, it gives animals a fright.
Why is there litter? It's not like glitter.

Recycling is right.
Pollution, there's no solution.

Amy Thornton (8)
St Joseph's Catholic Primary School, Keighley

Make Our World Supreme

Green, green, green machine
This world is not much a supreme.
War, war, what is all this for?
Litter, litter you make it glitter
Pollution, pollution that is not the solution
Extinction, extinction please do not pinch them
Recycle, recycle it makes the world better than a rusty old motorcycle.

Tegan Devlin (8)
St Joseph's Catholic Primary School, Keighley

The Lonely War

War, war,
What is it for?
People are fighting,
People are dying!
War is poor,
War is sore!
What is it used for?
It's getting bad,
It's getting sad!
People are dying,
People are crying!
It's not nice,
It's not kind!

Saira Ali (7)
St Joseph's Catholic Primary School, Keighley

Stop War

War, war, what is it for?
People are fighting,
People are dying,
I don't know why.
War, war, what is it for?
People are homeless,
I don't know why.
War, war, *stoooooooooop!*

Anthony Beckwith (7)
St Joseph's Catholic Primary School, Keighley

World Saving

I wish that there was no war.
So everybody could be friends.
I wish that there wasn't any climate change.
So the world would be a better place.
I wish that animal extinction stopped
Because it's not fair for the poor animals.
I wish that people were not homeless.
So everybody could be happy,
I wish that there was no pollution,
So the world could be a nicer place.
I wish these things could happen.
So the world would be a better place.

Hannah Greenwood (8)
St Joseph's Catholic Primary School, Keighley

A Good Place

Please, please do not smoke.
People fighting on the street.
People homeless, sitting on seats
People chucking rubbish on the floor
I wish the world was a better place.

Samantha Hinchcliffe (7)
St Joseph's Catholic Primary School, Keighley

Stop It War People

War, war, why can't you stop the war?
War, war, can you stop it, stop it
War people, please?

Kieron Blakeley (8)
St Joseph's Catholic Primary School, Keighley

Saving The World

Recycling, recycling everywhere
Cans and paper to melt down
Sometimes they don't sometimes they do,
It's not up to them, it's up to you!

War, war it should be a draw,
so we can all be friends
Sometimes we know it's hard but we can!

When animals die it makes me cry. That's why!

Niamh McGlynn (7)
St Joseph's Catholic Primary School, Keighley

Keep Our World Tidy

Smoke, smoke makes you choke
Green, green the big machine.
Homeless, homeless that is hopeless.
When animals die it makes me cry.

Ryan Ayers (8)
St Joseph's Catholic Primary School, Keighley

Recycling Saves The World

The world needs saving,
The world needs us,
Collect up the litter,
Start recycling to save the world,
Stop sunbathing,
The world needs saving,
Don't sit back relaxing,
The world is polluted,
So let's stop that now,
Recycling will save the world,
But the only way the world will be saved
Is if we start to recycle.

Sean Scully (11)
St Joseph's Catholic Primary School, Keighley

Racism

All the pain and hurt that's caused,
Please help to save us all,
There's more to life than different colours,
Please show that to others,
So don't fight, we'll make things right,
We'll be friends until the end.
If you've seen an awful sight,
Help us to make things right,
Stop racism!
Stop the fight.

Eve Kendall (11)
St Joseph's Catholic Primary School, Keighley

War Is Bad

W ar, war all day long,
A ll the innocent people gone,
R uined houses, blood-splattered walls.

C ivilians are killed for no reason at all,
A ll the violence near their homes,
N obody knows when it'll go.

K illing people isn't good,
I t can ruin all things good,
L et's stop it now!
L et's stop it now!

Sam Vickers (11)
St Joseph's Catholic Primary School, Keighley

Save The World

The world needs saving,
We can help.
So let's save it
Littering won't help.
Let's pick up all the litter
And do not waste our food.
Try to use less energy
And stop the gas fumes!
We can work together
We'll save the world forever.
Everyone can help.
Help your mother
Help your brother
All the nasty chemicals
Aren't going to help any of us
People crying for people dying.
We can make the world a better place
So let's help now
The world needs saving!

Emily McSharry (10)
St Joseph's Catholic Primary School, Keighley

War And Poverty

It's not that hard to just be friends,
War and poverty must come to an end,
People, people, can't you see,
That we are different, you and me.
If we work together, we'll make things right,
So look deep down and turn on a new light.
So remember, remember this little rhyme song,
Please, please, please drop love, not bombs.

Louise Evans (10)
St Joseph's Catholic Primary School, Keighley

Animals

Cutting down the rainforest is very mean and unkind,
Pandas will be gone forever if you don't decline,
Polar bears are dying because of global warming,
Please take this warning,
Stop now!

Niamh Hargreaves (11)
St Joseph's Catholic Primary School, Keighley

Save The Animals

Please save the animals.

Please make it stop!
There's no need to chop!
Our little tree friends,
So let's bring it to an end.

Please save the animals.
Don't forget the moles.
So when you use paper,
Remember these little souls.

Get rid of the guns!
Get rid of the saws!
Protect the Earth,
And the little paws.

Think what's right,
So don't be tight.
Save the animals,
Day and night.

Some animals are rare,
Some people don't care
So will you care?
Care!

Libby Cross (11)
St Joseph's Catholic Primary School, Keighley

Polar Bears

P lease read this poem,
O ver the Atlantic,
L ots of polar bears are dying,
A nd you must understand,
R eal problems are at hand,

B e good and kind,
E ven though you may find it hard,
A s putting down a family pet,
R eally it's just the same,
S o help them today.

Emily Harrison (11)
St Joseph's Catholic Primary School, Keighley

Racism!

Racism is wrong
It has gone on for too long

Black against white
White against black
On no, racism is back!

Chinese, American, Christian, Asian or Jamaican
Doesn't matter what race, we're all the same.

Come on now, help! Let's put it to a stop.
Yeah, we can all do this, if we all help put a stop to *racism!*

Nagina Ditta (11)
St Joseph's Catholic Primary School, Keighley

Litter

Litter here,
Litter there,
Litter it is everywhere!
Not in the bin,
But on the floor,
And stuck to the bottom of my shoe!
It's not nice,
But it is to the mice,
And to the repulsive rats as well.
But I have a thought,
Although it's two words,
Which are quite small.
It's
Bin it!
But if it is plastic or metal,
It really does depend.
Try and save our world,
By recycling it instead!

Terri Moseley (11)
St Joseph's Catholic Primary School, Keighley

Litter

And you're walking down a street,
And you're stamping your feet.
Then you hurt your hand,
All someone had to do
Was put it in the bin.

If it isn't in the bin
It will hurt someone else,
That's not very nice,
It can hurt animals too.

Amy De Belder (10)
St Joseph's Catholic Primary School, Keighley

Litter Less, Recycle More

Recycle, recycle,
Think of the world today,
Waste, waste,
Crisp packets, glass bottles and cans.
Litter, litter,
It's such a waste.
Recycle, recycle,
The possibilities are endless,
Waste, waste,
Carrier bags, grass and clothes.
Litter, litter,
Recycling saves the rainforest.
Recycle, recycle,
Your world needs your help.

Sophie Dearden (11)
St Joseph's Catholic Primary School, Keighley

Poverty All Around The World

The world is sad but we can make it glad
If we don't make a difference
To the litter and poverty.
The world will go mad!
The animals are going to be extinct
And then the world will stink.
We will have no love and trust in the world
Because all the people are falling apart.
The litter that people drop
Will have to be mopped up
When we could just crush it in the bin.
And people just mush their food in the ground
When it can be crushed in the bin
So nobody gets hurt!
Also the dirt is making the world reek.
We need to sort the world out!
Do your part and help!

Savannah Horsfall (11)
St Joseph's Catholic Primary School, Keighley

Global Warming

It's raining in the deserts,
It's hot in the Atlantic,
It's freezing in the summer,
It's making sea levels rise.
Having to cope with these ever changing conditions.
Our world is turning upside down!
Please walk to school every day,
If you can't do this then it's OK.
Try to use less energy,
Who knows, in time our world might end,
So let's try to save it
Now, now, now!

Hayley Kit (11)
St Joseph's Catholic Primary School, Keighley

Stop The War

Stop the war!
Stop the war!
Save the poor.

Stop the war!
Stop the war!
Follow the law.

Stop the war!
Stop the war!
We're all suffering.

Peace is the only thing we need!
If only you all agreed.

We want you to stop it
That's all we need!

Ihtisham Ahmed (10)
St Joseph's Catholic Primary School, Keighley

War Poem

War, war is such a bore
Let's settle the score
With war!
People die; people starve
While we drive around in fancy cars.

War, war is such a bore
Let's settle the score,
With war!
Let's help, let's go
And beat down our only foe.

Peace, peace,
Is what we need
It should be agreed it's what
We need!
Then we will help those who bleed.

Kye Plover (10)
St Joseph's Catholic Primary School, Keighley

Litter

Litter is bad
Some people go mad
When it's on the floor
It should be the law!
So pick it up now
Don't get in a fuss
If you have finished with a wrapper
Throw it in the bin, not on the floor
Remember *pick it up!*

Georgia Harrison (11)
St Joseph's Catholic Primary School, Keighley

War

War can be started over the smallest thing
But can end up disastrous
It costs lots of lives and can affect the world
By ruining farming land and can send a country into despair.
War is over the top
So it has to stop
If we all made peace
No more lives will be lost
On rare occasions war can be good
Just like World War II
But it wastes lots of money, which could be spent on the poor.

Lewis Feather (10)
St Joseph's Catholic Primary School, Keighley

Diseases

Diseases, diseases,
Coughs and sneezes,
Just a little something,
To cure this thing.

Diseases, diseases,
Coughs and sneezes,
Carry a handkerchief around with you,
Then people will copy you too.

Diseases, diseases,
Coughs and sneezes,
Cover your mouth with your hand,
Then it will be better for your land,

Diseases, diseases
Coughs and sneezes
We can make it stop right now!

Aneesa Parvais (10)
St Joseph's Catholic Primary School, Keighley

Bullying!

Bullying really is not nice,
Some people get bullied because of lice,
Some people get bullied because of their race,
So they move to a quieter different place,
Bullying is really unfair,
I wish that some people would care,
Bullies like to kick and punch,
Especially playtimes and lunch.

Jamie Sharples (11)
St Joseph's Catholic Primary School, Keighley

Go Green

Cars with petrol, cars with gas
Walk to school in a dash.

All the pollution in the air
To the animals, it's just not fair!

All the paper we use, it's just a disease
So use less and save our trees.

If you want to make our world shine like glitter
Get a bin and pick up litter

Soon our world will become a bore
All because of the useless war.

How do you feel? I don't know
So do your little bit and make it go.

So help the environment stay very safe,
And make our world a better place.

Kirstie Goodchild (8)
St Joseph's Catholic Primary School, Keighley

Help The Environment

Don't throw litter on the floor,
And don't let people go to war.
With all the pollution in the air,
Some people do not care.
Help us all go so far,
Recycle everything you can.
All of the rainforests are being cut down,
And sold around all over town.
So stop, stop, stop all this mess,
And our country will be the best!

Keep the world green and clean!

Chloe Carr (8)
St Joseph's Catholic Primary School, Keighley

Save The Country

To the environment
It's not fair
With all the pollution
In the air
We need to clean up the country
And pick up stuff
And clean up after ourselves
And put rubbish in the bins.

Jennie-Lee Roberts (7)
St Joseph's Catholic Primary School, Keighley

Little Miss Bird

Little Miss Bird
Had a word
With the environment
They want to stop it
To stop the war
To stop the pollution
And the poverty
And littering the streets
We want to save the animals
And the rainforests
And do recycling.

Katie Nash (8)
St Joseph's Catholic Primary School, Keighley

The Big Green Poetry Machine

I am the eco-kid.
I put litter in the bin.
Help save the animals.
Help stop the pollution from killing us.
Don't bin it, recycle it.
Stop the people going to war.
Also help the people that are poor.
The people who smoke make the pollution in the air.
Reduce, reuse, recycle!

Max Moseley (8)
St Joseph's Catholic Primary School, Keighley

Stop, Stop!

Walk instead of drive
So bees can make their hives
Stop shooting birds
They haven't done anything wrong
They're just flying and they're free
To do anything they like.
Don't dump things in the lakes for goodness sake
You'll just cause pollution.

Ryan Henry (8)
St Joseph's Catholic Primary School, Keighley

Save Our Planet

Hello, I am the Eco-kid.
To help the animals and the environment.
Please do not cut the trees down.
Pollution can spread to us and animals.
Recycle bottles, plastic and paper.
Pick up litter, into the bin.
Stop, stop, stop, don't drop litter.
It will become a dirty world.

Taylor Hardaker (8)
St Joseph's Catholic Primary School, Keighley

The Environment Poem

Help the environment
By not throwing rubbish on the floor.
Please stop wars in all the countries.
Recycle all the things you can
Plastic and glass and bottles
To help the environment and people
Please stop littering!

Bill Narey (8)
St Joseph's Catholic Primary School, Keighley

Our Planet And Us

The animals die slowly
Falling to the ground
Others very ill
Water rising, animals drowning.

Look around your world
Temperatures rising, higher
Life is dying as we talk
Pollution is killing our life.

Number of animals
Dropping down quickly
Throwing rubbish on the floor
Swept into the ocean.

Extinction, dying
Animals crying
Whimpering, sad
This is all our fault.

You can make a difference
To our dying world
Recycle, reuse and reduce
It's all down to you.

Sophie Kershaw (11)
Towngate Primary School, Ossett

Walk Alone

A wild animal walks alone
Unaware of the things that
Might happen
To the poor
Creature
Of God's
Beautiful
Earth!
A bullet
Could enter
Its body
The fire could
Burn its soul for
The world is warming
We could all die like the poor
Creature that walks alone!

Ben Cornell (11)
Towngate Primary School, Ossett

Be Green!

We need to get the message across,
To save the Earth and be keen,
About what is going on with the planet,
Do your bit and be green!

Reuse, repair, reduce and recycle,
The four Rs,
To help to cut down rubbish and landfill sites,
Paper, tins and jars.

In another eighty years,
It will be horrible and you won't know how,
The world will be full of gases,
That's why we need to act now!

Daisy Kennedy (11)
Towngate Primary School, Ossett

Rainforests Need Help

Trees are all around,
Animals hiding away,
But we need to help,
As it is dying away.

Habitats destroyed,
Animals losing their homes,
But we need to help,
For they will exit our world.

But that is not all,
Polluting all our fresh air,
But we need to help,
Look what we've done to our world.

Certain things need help,
The rainforests on the list,
But we need to help,
So what does everyone think?

Jessica Allatt (11)
Towngate Primary School, Ossett

Racism

Whether you're black, whether you're white,
Whether you're fat or really skinny
We need to stop
Racism,
We all have a place in this world,
If you have curly hair or straight
It really doesn't matter
Just what you are
So we need to stop
Racism
Just stop and help beat
Racism today
And let's start straight away.

Kate Priestley (10)
Towngate Primary School, Ossett

Pollution

Car exhaust fumes galore
Will this ever end?
Global warming, polar ice caps
Will this ever end?

Oceans rising washing up on your shore
Tips are overfilling
Where does it all go?
Polluting the air everywhere.

What is this all coming to?
Why is it all happening now?
Could it be because of us?
What's going to happen now?

Pollution, global warming,
These are all Man's disasters
Please say you've done your part
And you could do a lot of repair.

Landfills can take no more
Tips filled to the brim
You better start recycling
Or you could lose your skin.

Joseph Exley (10)
Towngate Primary School, Ossett

Eco-Poem

Ignorant people
Being so mean
Help cause global warming
By increasing the gauge on a washing machine.

They are throwing litter on the ground
They are turning up their heating
Their cars are causing carbon emissions
They are not really thinking.

Lives are being lost,
But so many could be spared
Polar bears, penguins,
If people only cared.

Today's tins and cans are tomorrow's vans,
Today's garden waste and apple cores are next week's compost.

So do your part for climate change
Look before you leap,
Reduce, reuse, repair, recycle
Put our world at ease!

Jessica Taylor (11)
Towngate Primary School, Ossett

Green Poem

Cans, bottles, doesn't matter
What type?
Let's see you doing
Your bit every time.

Reduce, reuse, repair, recycle
You know you want to
It's very good so let's try.

Paper, glass every time
Let's see you in such time
So let's try and save our
Environment
So we can have a good time.

Nicola Fox (10)
Towngate Primary School, Ossett

Global Warming

Global warming, global warming,
Is destroying our world,
It is melting the ice,
And isn't very nice.

The weather's getting warmer,
It's going a bit too far,
But you could make a difference
Just cycle instead of using the car!

Emma Bolton (11)
Towngate Primary School, Ossett

Big Green Poetry Machine

In a wild animals' paradise,
The animals are free
They're always running here and there
As happy as can be.

But one day there was a loud noise
The animals looked up
And there towering over them,
Was a huge mechanical truck.

The animals were worried
The animals were scared
Some fled their homes
Some stayed and fought.

The ones that fled
Were fine for the present
They looked upon the world they left
The families that they lost.

Megan Downes (11)
Towngate Primary School, Ossett

Litter

Litter on the floor I think
We all could do a little bit more.

It's everywhere we need to stop it
But no one cares.
I think it annoys people
So let's stop it now.

To stop this we need to work together,
If we don't stop now
It will carry on forever.

The people of the world keep doing it,
It's litter galore and
It's breaking the law.

Even though people keep doing it more and more
But really we need to save our floor.

Repair our world by stopping littering
So why don't you
Reduce, reuse, recycle
Everywhere?

Lauren Ekert (10)
Towngate Primary School, Ossett

Distressed Animal

A poor animal distressed and annoyed,
With all those hunting for joy.
Scared as he creeps around,
A bang then a howl,
What could be waiting over there?
Deep enemies walking around,
Seeing what they can find,
By prowling around.

Lewys Irvin (11)
Towngate Primary School, Ossett

Recycle

Recycle, recycle,
Anything you want
If it is paper or tin.

Next thing you know,
Your tin is a plane
Or a nice super car.

Recycle, recycle,
Anything you want
If it is paper or tin.

Next thing you know,
Your paper could be
Your next newspaper.

Recycle, recycle,
Anything you want
If it is paper or tin
Recycle.

Alex Coy (11)
Towngate Primary School, Ossett

Rubbish - Cinquain

Litter
Affects people
Rivers getting messy
It is horribly awful
Rubbish.

Phoebe Shore (9), Ella Lamming & Katie Malik (8)
Towngate Primary School, Ossett

In The Rainforest - Cinquain

Birds sing
Ants in your pants
Climbing monkeys in trees
Butterflies are flying about
Birds fly.

Natalia King & Luke England (9)
Towngate Primary School, Ossett

Homeless

Homes
Homeless
Poor people
Don't have
Homes.

Shannon McGroggan (9) & Bethany Wilbert (8)
Towngate Primary School, Ossett

Rainforest - Cinquain

Help us!
Love the nature
Poor kids in the forest
Help the children in rainforests
Thank you!

Sam Hewitt & Ryan Strafford (9)
Towngate Primary School, Ossett

I Hate Global Warming

I
Don't like
Pollution
It melts the ice
And Antarctica
Stop going out in cars!
They pollute the atmosphere
And it will kill the animals
That's why we don't like global warming
I want to stop people polluting ice.

Adam Wheeler & Harry Strafford (8)
Towngate Primary School, Ossett

Rainforest Pollution

Don't
Pollute
Rainforests
It is horrid
It is disgusting
It is not nice
Please do stop
Stop it
Yuck!

Molly Maw (8) & Natalie Gregson (9)
Towngate Primary School, Ossett

Diseases

Ill
Poorness
Medicine
Dying
Dead.

Arran Senior, Holly Saynor & Jaya Sharma (9)
Towngate Primary School, Ossett

Rainforest

Rain
Water
In a row
Periwinkle
Alligators swim
Birds sitting on a tree.

Chloe Stanley, Kelsey Lambourn & Emily Hudson (9)
Towngate Primary School, Ossett

Recycling

Recycling is good
It is good for our health
We want to recycle a lot
So it saves our world
Recycling is apple pie
But please recycle a lot
You can recycle glass, paper, plastic
It makes the world fantastic
It is good for the world
I recycle a lot
I hope you do too
Or the world will smell.

Chloe Smith (7)
Towngate Primary School, Ossett

Recycling

Recycling is good
It's good for the Earth
And good for your health.
Recycling is fun for everyone.
You can touch your toes
But please read this rhyme
Please do it, it's so fantastic.
Recycling is fun for everyone.
You can recycle paper and plastic
To make the world fantastic.

Samuel Beaumont (8)
Towngate Primary School, Ossett

Recycling

Recycling, recycling,
Recycling's good.
If you keep it up you'll have a happy universe.
If you want a better environment keep on recycling.
So keep on recycling to have a better world.
Recycling's spreading happiness all over.

Sean Owram (8)
Towngate Primary School, Ossett

Recycling

Recycling is good.
Recycling will save the planet.
You can recycle plastic and paper.
You can recycle bubble bath and chocolate boxes.
It will make the Earth fantastic.
Recycling is as easy as pie.
Recycling is better than sitting down.
Recycling is fun.
All you have to do is find a recycling box.
People do not want to smell the bin.
It is good to recycle.
If you don't, the world will smell.

Harmony Tavakoli (8)
Towngate Primary School, Ossett

Recycling

Recycling means to have a think.
Just think how the world would stink.
People are recycling in many places.
That means there are lots of happy faces.
You can recycle plastic bottles and banana peel.
You can even recycle metal shields.
If you recycle you could buy a knife.
Just think you could be saving someone's life.

Abigail Hemingway (8)
Towngate Primary School, Ossett

Recycling

When you recycle you save the universe and people's lives.
If you recycle you're a superhero.
You can recycle bottles, silver things, glass, paper,
Food peelings and plastic.
There are different kinds of bins,
Green bin, paper bin and a garden bin.
I will not give up recycling, will you?
So please help save the world by recycling.
So recycle.

Ella Walker (8)
Towngate Primary School, Ossett

Recycling

R ecycling is great.
E veryone can do it.
C ans can be recycled
Y ou can recycle anything.
C arrot peel, potato peel.
L isten to me.
I t is fun.
N ever stop recycling.
G randma, Grandad, Mum, Dad, everyone can recycle.

Rebecca Hobson & Joshua Callaghan (8)
Towngate Primary School, Ossett

Recycling Poem

Recycling is an invention thought of many years ago,
When you recycle you save our planet,
It's just space junk too,
But let's sort the biggest problem first,
Recycling is so easy and fun.
Recycling in lots of places and see lots of happy faces.
Rubbish is like a mountain growing day by day.
You can recycle glass, metal and even tins,
Recycling means to find out what you need to know,
Don't let rubbish grow.
Recycling means to go with a flow
Recycle please and help me grow!

Bethany Cooper (8)
Towngate Primary School, Ossett

Recycling

Recycling means
Putting things in the recycling box
Instead of the bins
You can recycle
Bottles, boxes and tins
It is fun to recycle
It will make the world fantastic
Recycling is fun for everyone.

Jordan Grace (8)
Towngate Primary School, Ossett

Recycling

Start recycling now,
If you are recycling you are an eco-warrior;
Or you can start recycling by putting all your paper bags in one box
And tins and glasses in another box.
It's easy, so start recycling now.

Kelsey Johnson (9)
Towngate Primary School, Ossett

Recycle

R euse things
E nergy needs to be saved
C lean all litter up
Y ou need to help save the environment
C lean environment we want
L et's all recycle
E veryone help.

Alana King (10)
Towngate Primary School, Ossett

Recycling

I live in a waste dump,
There's cardboard and paper just lying around.
In our lovely green field there's rubbish around.
In our town there's litter bugs that don't care what's on the ground.
Plastic and cardboard, pots and pans near the grass in the park
where we walk and play catch.
Please I don't like it, I don't understand, but when I went to school
one day I learnt about recycling.
You put cardboard and plastic in a special green bin
and bottles in the green box to help the environment.
When I got home I couldn't stop recycling,
putting things in the special green bin, now everyone recycles!
I live in a town
a beautiful town where there's flowers and meadows to see.
Beautiful smells, lovely fresh air!
Nowhere happier to be.

Darcie Hill (9)
Towngate Primary School, Ossett

Paper, Tin, Plastic, Glass

Paper, tin, plastic, glass
All have a recycling bin's pass
Paper can be used again
Loo roll and wrapping paper is a gain.

Paper, tin, plastic, glass
All have a recycling bin's pass
Tin can have a long course
To provide a powerful energy source.

Paper, tin, plastic, glass
All have a recycling bin's pass
Plastic can be melted down
And made into things around the town.

Paper, tin, plastic, glass
All have a recycling bin's pass
Glass can break and crack and smash
But remember not to put it in the trash.

Nathan Wilby (9)
Towngate Primary School, Ossett

Recycling, Recycling

Recycling, recycling
Make the world green
Recycling, recycling
Should always be seen!

Kieran Shields (10)
Towngate Primary School, Ossett

The Silhouette Of The War-Path

The silhouette of the war-path
Gets shined on each evening as the sun sets

The silhouette of death
That's the only thing to see
On the dark war-path
The heroes that have tried so hard
Watch the never-ending day

For those people that try so hard
The valiant and brave
The strong and courageous
To save others and the world

We watch them trying
In the silhouette of the war-path.

Molly Strafford (10)
Towngate Primary School, Ossett

Recycling

R is the 'R' in reuse, reduce and repair.
E is the 'E' in environment and ecological.
C is the 'C' in creating a better world.
Y is the 'Y' in yearning for everyone to recycle.
C is the 'C' in cleaning the mess mankind has made.
L is the 'L' in learning about recycling.
I is the 'I' in introducing recycling.
N is the 'N' in natural resources.
G is the 'G' in a greener world.

Benjamin Black (10)
Towngate Primary School, Ossett

Recycling

Recycling, recycling it is fun
It's not hard, just pull out a thumb.
If you do there will be fun
So come on, let's have some now.
You have got a wheelie bin so come on let's put stuff out.

Recycling, recycling it is fun
It's not hard just pull out a thumb.
Everybody give it a try,
You can recognise in no time.
Everybody do it now, so then the world can shine.

Alexander Remmer (9)
Towngate Primary School, Ossett

Recycle

Recycle, recycle, recycle paper, card and tins
Recycle, recycle, recycle we're baffled with all these bins
Recycle, recycle, recycle our planet we're hoping to save
Recycle, recycle, recycle we'd be better off living in a cave.

Liam Senior (10)
Towngate Primary School, Ossett

Recycle

Reuse things by recycling,
It helps nature.
Just recycle your old cans and bottles,
And you will save our ozone layer.
Anything can be recycled,
It's easy to recycle,
Just reduce and reuse.
We can help our world to be cleaner
So recycle, recycle!

Luke Churchill (10)
Towngate Primary School, Ossett

Endangered Animals

Elephants wandering through the sand
Paddling and waddling, ears so grand
Tigers hiding from the big fierce hunters
Next they're on a lady's jumper.
Polar bears floating away on ice
Because of the big nasty monsters
Whales searching for food
Next they're on a dinner plate
Koalas climb up high
Next they die!

Emma Heslington (11)
Weaverthorpe CE Primary School, Malton

Ze Good, Ze Bad

Ze good - Cornwall
People walk on short journeys,
Not that much pollution.
Really peaceful place,
No jam-packed roads.
Woods and green scenery.

Ze bad - London
People drive on short journeys,
Loads of pollution.
Noisy streets,
Jam-packed roads.
Flats and houses everywhere.

Alex Rough (10) & Louis Hopper (9)
Weaverthorpe CE Primary School, Malton

Polar Bears

Polar bears are endangered because of us
If you don't turn your lights off
And drive your car when you don't need to
Because it makes global warming
When you go in the car
Remember what's at risk!

James Ireland (9)
Weaverthorpe CE Primary School, Malton

Poverty And Recycling - Haikus

Cutting down the trees
A very horrible sight
Unnecessary

Let us save today
Save paper and metal it's
Fantabbytossy.

Mollie Beresford (8)
Weaverthorpe CE Primary School, Malton

Turning Off

Turning the lights off.
Turning the computer off.
Turning the SmartBoard off.
Turning the TV off.
Turning the heaters off.
Turning the tap off.
Turning the laptop off.
Turning the video player off.

Georgia Tiffany (9)
Weaverthorpe CE Primary School, Malton

Endangered Animals

Toads in the roads, did not see the lights ahead
And now they're marked with tyre treads.
Pandas taken to Uganda, did not see the hunters behind them.
Snakes put in crates, did not see the hands of a man coming
                                                    to get them.
Fish put on a cutting table, did not see the net, I bet!

Maisie Thomson (10)
Weaverthorpe CE Primary School, Malton

Planting A Seed

Plant a seed, it's easy to do
Grow some veg,
But make sure it's right for you!
Don't fancy veg?
Plant some flowers
You will be in the garden for hours and hours . . .
Wait until May, flowers bright.
Seeds shoot up.
Looking pretty all through the night.
So just plant a seed.
Just try, go ahead!
You will end up with a beautiful flowerbed.

Katie Botterill (10)
Weaverthorpe CE Primary School, Malton

Animals

You should not shoot birds,
You should feed them,
A cute and cuddly panda,
The numbers of them are going down,
You can save them by not killing them.

Phoebe Pickering (8)
Weaverthorpe CE Primary School, Malton

The Poem

You can turn off the TV and save hundreds of animals every day.
You can save the habitat
Do not take the car, take the bike!
Don't run away or you will pay!

Megan Stubbings (9)
Weaverthorpe CE Primary School, Malton

Cycling

If you're only going up the hill.
Get your bike and ride up the hill.
Cycle to school
Not drive to school
Then you can save the animals.
If you live near the school
Get a group of friends and cycle
Cycle
Cycle
Cycle.

Gabriella Fisher (10)
Weaverthorpe CE Primary School, Malton

Tears Of Terror

War, why?
Fighting,
Killing,
Capturing,
Destroying,
Bombs,
Guns,
Slaughtering,
Hurtful, heartless,
Bloodshed,
Murder,
Raid,
Attack!
Tears of sorrow
And
Terror.

Philippa Launchbury (9)
Wold Newton School, Driffield

Mother Nature

Maybe black, maybe white
They both hunt in the night.
Bullets here, bullets there,
Illegal hunting everywhere.
A world of death, slaughter and pollution,
When will these killers get their retribution?
Mother Nature.

Richard Bannister (10)
Wold Newton School, Driffield

Litter

If you throw your junk on the floor,
It may get stuck on an animal's claw,
Landfills are polluting the Earth,
Is this all your planet is worth?
Littering makes a mark on our planet,
Now it's time to finally ban it.

Recycle now!

Billy Garbutt (10)
Wold Newton School, Driffield

Pollution

Pollution! Make it stop:
Stop the war against people:
Stop making explosive weapons:
Stop the factories and their black smoke:
Stop the slaughter of animals in our litter:
Stop the bad health.

Start the war against pollution.
Start making eco-friendly cars.
Start recycling all your rubbish.
Start taking care of our environment.

John Collier-Woods (9)
Wold Newton School, Driffield

Young Writers Information

We hope you have enjoyed reading this book - and that you will continue to enjoy it in the coming years.

If you like reading and writing poetry drop us a line, or give us a call, and we'll send you a free information pack.

Alternatively if you would like to order further copies of this book or any of our other titles, then please give us a call or log onto our website at www.youngwriters.co.uk

**Young Writers Information
Remus House
Coltsfoot Drive
Peterborough
PE2 9JX**

(01733) 890066